D0505739

Warrior
The first modern battleship

Walter Brownlee
MASTER MARINER

Drawings by John E. Wigston

1986

CAMBRIDGE UNIVERSITY PRESS
Cambridge
London   New York   New Rochelle
Melbourne   Sydney

Published by the Press Syndicate of the University of Cambridge
The Pitt Building, Trumpington Street, Cambridge CB2 1RP
32 East 57th Street, New York, NY 10022, USA
10 Stamford Road, Oakleigh, Melbourne 3166, Australia

First published 1985

Printed in Hong Kong by Wing King Tong

Library of Congress catalogue card number: 84-45842

British Library cataloguing in publication data
Brownlee, Walter
Warrior – (Cambridge introduction to the history of mankind:
Topic book)
1. Warrior (*ship*) – Juvenile literature
I. Title
359.3'2'250941   VA458.W/
ISBN 0 521 27579 2

Measurements
In this book the dimensions of ships and fittings are those in use at the
time *Warrior* was built. For consistency and ease of reading no
measurements have been metricated.

The author and publisher would like to thank the following for permission to reproduce illustrations:

front cover, pp 7, 26r, 27, 30b, 32b, 35t, 41tl, 44 The National
Maritime Museum, Greenwich, London; pp 3, 9l, 10l, 16, 30t, 33b
Mary Evans Picture Library; pp 4, 5l, 6l, 9r, 11l, 12b, 48 British
Crown Copyright, Science Museum, London; p 6r The Black Watch
Regimental Headquarters for *Wreck of HMS 'Birkenhead'* by
Thomas M. Hemy, 1892; pp 12t, 41br The Royal Institute of Naval
Architects; p 15 Royal Artillery Regimental Museum; pp 17b, 40r
from *Punch*, reproduced by permission of the Syndics of Cambridge
University Library; pp 17t, 41tr, 42tl, 43tr, Imperial War Museum;
pp 28, 29 © John Fabb from *Victorian and Edwardian Navy*
(Batsford); p 32t Mrs Alderman; p 38 from Edward M. Miller,
USS 'Monitor' (Leeward Publications Inc.); pp 39t, 42bl, 43br, 47b,
back cover Ships Preservation Trust Ltd, Hartlepool; p 39b
Glenview Studios; p 41bl from F.T. Jane, *The British Battlefleet*
(1912) reproduced by permission of the Syndics of Cambridge
University Library; p 42tr, br, 43tl, 45, 46tr Dave Morrel; p 43bl
Keith Johnson; p 47t Crown Copyright Reserved, Fleet Photo-
graphic Unit, Portsmouth.

**To all the members, past and present, of the restoration team
and work force at Hartlepool, County Cleveland.**

'I often wonder how I mustered sufficient courage to order
the construction of such a novel vessel.'

Sir John Pakington, 1860

'I often wonder how I mustered sufficient courage to
undertake it.'

Reply to Sir John by builder, 1860

'I wonder how I had the courage to undertake what has
turned out to be the largest ship restoration to date.'

Ray Hockey, Project Director, 1982

front cover: *'Warrior' in 1861, a colour lithograph by
J.T. Dutton.*
*Dutton shows 'Warrior' under both sail and steam power.
The main sails of the fore and main masts are furled to prevent
charring by the coal smoke and to allow a passage of free air
around the funnels. The small royal yards carried at the very
top of each mast have not been set. All the other yards have
been hauled well round to catch the wind, which is a few
points on the port bow. She flies the Red Ensign, since the
three-squadron system (the Red, the White and the Blue) was
in use until August 1864: after that date all Royal Navy ships
flew the White Ensign.*
*Although this lithograph is the earliest picture of 'Warrior'
under sail, it must be noted that Dutton was selling copies of
the picture before she had finished her fitting out, so he can-
not have seen the ship exactly as he has pictured her.*

back cover: *This stained and torn fragment was discovered in
1983 among the effects of Captain Cochrane, 'Warrior's' first
captain, 1862–4. It shows a section of the ship through the
boiler room. The simple boilers are fed from the central alley;
beyond them are the bunkers, shown full of coal and with their
coal trolleys visible. Wing tanks flank the bunkers and rise up
to enclose the lower deck with its bag racks. The main deck is
shown with two 68-pounders; the gunport lid raising gear is
shown above the left gun. On the upper deck there is a section
through the bulwark, topped by its hammock rack. The armour
plates, coloured blue, are shown bolted through the layers of
teak to the ship's side.*

title page: *HMS 'Warrior' – completed September 1862. No
other navy in the world could boast a warship as large as
'Warrior' until 1869, when the North German Confederation
obtained the slightly larger 'König Wilhelm', built by the
Thames Iron Works who had built 'Warrior' nine years earlier.*

Contents

'Warrior' under construction, 1859. 'Warrior' was constantly in the news during her construction and the periodicals of the day carried regular reports on her progress. This is an artist's view, printed in 'The Illustrated London News', showing the bottom of the vertical tunnel which housed the propeller when not in use (see p. 10). The size of 'Warrior' was overwhelming, and reporters attempted to create the same impression in print, so here the artist has reduced the size of the people to make the ship appear huge. Unfortunately he overdid it; when the people are compared with the draught marks (the Roman numerals on the stern post) they are found to be only two feet high!

1 Prelude to change

A great tradition

When Victoria came to the throne in 1837, Britain led the world in two ways. She was the first industrialised country, increasingly rich despite the squalor of some of the expanding manufacturing cities; and she was the greatest sea power, with a navy that had won its proud position during the long struggle against Napoleon and now kept the world's seaways safe for commerce. Patriotic Britons gloried in 'ruling the waves', while sober statesmen knew that without naval supremacy their trading prosperity would be at risk and they would not be able to prevent invasion from across the Channel – France was still the leading military power in Europe, and Britain's traditional foe.

Their Lordships of the Admiralty were responsible for everything to do with the Royal Navy: organisation, supplies, ships and men. Their system had brought triumph, and it would be folly to upset this. Change might cause confusion and encourage foreign rivals. Yet it was important not to miss genuine improvements, for such neglect might also give rivals an opportunity. So the Admiralty looked at proposed innovations, but very, very, cautiously.

In the decades after Trafalgar they permitted some changes in their 'wooden walls'. Bows and sterns, always the most vulnerable parts, were built stronger and plainer; a system of cross-bracing made the construction of hulls more firm; iron angle pieces began to replace the massive wooden 'knees' that held beams together. The size of ships gradually increased. But these were mere details, and the ships of the line remained as they had been for a hundred years, with towering masts, billowing sails and rows of guns thrusting from oaken sides. It would take very strong arguments to persuade the Admiralty to budge from what had served so nobly in the past.

But pressure of new ideas was becoming insistent.

Steam power

Unlike the Admiralty, enterprising merchant shipowners were trying out new ways to improve speed, strength and carrying capacity. The first successful experiments in using steam to propel boats took place in France, Britain and America in the late eighteenth century, and steam boats went into commercial service at the beginning of the nineteenth. In 1807 the American Robert Fulton was running a paddle steamer service on the Hudson River, in 1812 Henry Bell's *Comet* sailed on the Clyde between Greenock and Glasgow, and in 1816 the English Channel was crossed by a paddle steamer. During the 1820s the rivers of Europe were being churned by steam-powered paddles fitted in small vessels and their use in deep-water ships was growing. In 1837, after a few attempts, each more successful than the last, the first reliable trans-Atlantic paddle steamer service was set in motion by Isambard Kingdom Brunel with his *Great Western*. The age of deep-sea steam power had arrived unmistakably in the year that Queen Victoria was crowned.

The 'Great Western', 1837. This was the first paddle steamer specifically designed for regular trans-Atlantic passenger and cargo service.
   Speed, 10 knots; length 236 feet; beam 35 feet; boiler pressure from four boilers, 5 pounds per square inch; paddle diameter, 28.75 feet.
   She was masted and rigged for sails, because neither the engines nor the supply of coal for the boilers could be relied upon completely.

Paddles in the Royal Navy

The Admiralty's attitude to paddle power in warships was clear from the beginning. No ship of the line would be fitted with paddles. The space taken by the engine and paddle mechanism would reduce the space available for guns by at least one third, and since the whole point of the large ship of the line was to present massive fire power it was considered ridiculous to fit paddles. It was sensibly noted that a single shot could shatter a paddle and leave a warship helpless.

However for small frigates and sloops there was a possible use; and there was a definite need for small paddle boats to act as tugs in confined waters. So in 1822 the Royal Navy received its first paddle tug and this was followed by another twelve in the next few years.

A paddle frigate, 1845. The number of wooden paddle warships built or converted in the Royal Navy was 12 frigates, about 30 sloops, and about 100 small boats of various sizes. This contemporary print shows HMS 'Terrible', built in 1845, a typical 20-gun frigate. She is under both sail and steam power, with her main sail furled to avoid scorching by the smoke. Seamen accustomed to sailing ships called these steamers 'Stinking Billies'. To the right is a first-rate ship of the line – its structure hardly changed from the days of the Napoleonic Wars, forty years before.

The first paddle boats involved in action were the *Diana* in Rangoon and the *Lightning* off Algeria, both in 1824. Between 1824 and 1852 eighteen wooden paddle frigates were built, but none carried more than 21 guns, and twelve carried only 6 guns.

Screw propulsion

The development of screw (propeller) propulsion had been delayed by a technical problem – the need to pierce the hull below the waterline. This was overcome, and in 1839 Pettit Smith demonstrated his SS (Screw Ship) *Archimedes*. The Admiralty were impressed – but did nothing. An interested observer, I.K. Brunel, was also impressed and he acted at once. He was building an iron-hulled paddle steamer, but he changed her to a screw ship. In 1845 the SS *Great Britain* made her outstandingly successful maiden voyage across the Atlantic, and the Admiralty began to take the matter seriously.

Outside pressure now forced them into action. France, ruled by Napoleon's nephew, Napoleon III, began to challenge British sea supremacy and in 1850 built the *Napoleon*, a screw-propelled ship of the line. Britain responded by converting HMS *Sans Pareil* to screw power. By 1858 Britain had 32 screw-driven ships of the line. However the French also built or converted 32 ships. The determination of France to become a great sea power was beginning to worry the Admiralty.

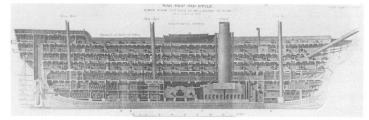

Section through a screw-propelled ship of the line, 1852. She is simply a wooden three decker fitted with boilers, engines and bunkers. This arrangement was acceptable to the Admiralty since the machinery was all below the waterline and well protected. The funnel is on the centre line so does not interfere with the rows of guns and the propeller can be hauled up into the hull when the ship is under sail alone.

Many seamen noted that the weight of machinery in these wooden ships made the vessel sag in the middle.

Iron hulls

The development of iron-hulled vessels progressed against a background of disbelief and scorn. Many refused to believe that iron ships would float; others thought that they would sink in seconds if holed.

The first notable iron ship was the *Aaron Manby*, 1821, and after 1830 many more followed, until the maritime world's attention was focused on the *Great Britain*, 1843, the first iron-hulled screw-propelled vessel to cross the Atlantic. Until 1859 it was the Merchant Navy that led the way in iron ships. They found that such ships were stronger than wooden ones, could withstand stranding, and, more important, there was no apparent limit to their size. Brunel illustrated this dramatically in 1858 when he produced his giant *Great Eastern*, 680 feet long and 70 feet wide, the largest ship the world had ever seen.

The Admiralty made a brief experiment. In 1845 they built five iron-hulled frigates, the *Birkenhead* and *Trident* being the first, and then in 1849 their largest, *Simoon*, 246 feet long.

SS 'Great Britain', designed and built by I.K. Brunel at Bristol. She was launched in 1843 by Prince Albert, and fitted out in London. In calm water her speed was 11 knots and her hull was divided into six watertight compartments. With a length of 322 feet she could carry 360 passengers. She made her maiden voyage across the Atlantic in July 1845; Liverpool to New York in 14 days 21 hours despite gale force head winds. She demonstrated clearly the advantage of iron hulls and screw propulsion. Now more and more merchant ships were built with iron hulls.

However, tests ashore showed that shot from a standard naval gun either passed straight through the iron plates or else shattered them into deadly flying fragments of jagged metal. As a result, in 1850 the official policy was that iron was quite unsuitable for use in warships, and the Navy's existing iron ships were either sold or converted to transports. The major naval nations of the world accepted the British findings; all, that is, except France.

The loss of the 'Birkenhead'. The 'Birkenhead' was the first iron-hulled frigate built by the Royal Navy in 1845, but she was soon altered to become a transport ship. In January 1852 she left for South Africa carrying a detachment of the 74th Highlanders, 487 officers and men accompanied by their wives and children. The vessel struck a rock off Danger Point near Cape Town on the morning of 26 February and began to settle rapidly.

This Victorian painting represents the heroism and tragedy of the occasion. The troops stood fast in ranks on the deck to allow the women and children to fill the lifeboats – 454 men were lost. The incident inspired many poems and paintings. It was popularly felt that had she been made of wood she might have sunk less quickly or remained afloat, and the tragedy would have been averted. For many years this incident engendered a mistrust of iron ships, even though an enquiry revealed that the ship's internal partitions, which would perhaps have enabled her to stay afloat, had been cut during her conversion to a troopship.

2 Forcing the changes

Gloire

In France on 1 January 1857 the designer and constructor Dupuy de Lôme was appointed Directeur du Matériel. He halted all construction of wooden ships of the line and produced plans for a new French fleet. In March 1858 the first six ships were ordered – *Gloire, Invincible, Normandie, Couronne, Magenta* and *Solferino*. Dupuy de Lôme had intended the new fleet to be all iron hulled, but French industry was not yet capable of producing on such a large scale; so the first three ships had to have wooden hulls but armoured with solid wrought iron plates. *Gloire* was launched on 24 November 1859, after about twenty months of construction, and was completed in August 1860.

Gloire was not Dupuy de Lôme's dream of perfection, but she was safe from the attacks of any British ship. With her speed of nearly 13 knots she could chase the British fleet out of the Channel.

British reaction

In May 1858 intelligence reports reached Britain revealing the French plans. The press over-reacted, war rumours spread, the public demanded that something be done. On 28 June the Surveyor to the Admiralty reported:

'. . . it is not in the interests of Great Britain . . . to adopt any important change in the construction of a new class of very costly vessels, until such a course is forced upon her by the adoption of a foreign power of formidable ships of a novel character requiring similar ships to cope with them . . . This time has arrived. France has now commenced to build frigates of great speed with their sides protected by thick metal plates, and this renders it imperative for this country to do the same without a moment's delay.'

Many in the Admiralty wanted simply to clad British ships with iron plates but the first Lord, Sir John Pakington, argued for a bolder response – an iron ship with iron armour. Backed by the Chief Constructor Isaac Watts and the designer John Scott Russell, he won the day. On 29 April 1859 tenders were called for and that of Ditchburn and Mare (later called the Thames Iron Works) of Blackwall was accepted. The keel was laid down on 25 May 1859.

Britain had decided to build what was to be the fastest, largest, strongest most powerful warship in the world.

'Gloire', a contemporary print. Dupuy de Lôme produced the most revolutionary warship the world had ever seen, which could pound the sides of a 120-gun wooden ship with impunity. 'Gloire' could be said to be the 'Father of Warrior'.

Ordered 4 March 1858; laid down March 1858; launched 24 November 1859; completed August 1860.

Length 256 feet; breadth 55¾ feet; draught 25 feet; displacement 5618 tons; cost £243,000; complement about 550 men; speed about 13 knots; 34 guns on main deck, 2 on upper deck; gunports 6–7 feet above waterline, 4 feet wide.

Armour: wrought iron plates 4.7 inches thick at gunport level and 4.3 inches at waterline, all backed by 26 inches of wood; an armoured conning tower protected by 4-inch plates on the upper deck.

Revolutionary concepts

A glance at *Warrior* suggests a typical frigate of the 1840s – a sailing ship with auxiliary steam power, a row of broadside guns and the low, fast, silhouette of a free-roving fifth-rate. But her design was based on new principles.

First build a box . . .

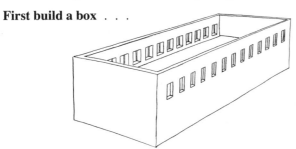

At least thirteen of her large guns on each side were to be 15 feet apart and enclosed within an armoured fort – the citadel. To eliminate the old danger of raking shot, which could smash in a stern and sweep the length of the gun deck, the ends of the box were closed. This box-like fort formed the central impervious core of the ship.

. . . then add the ends . . .

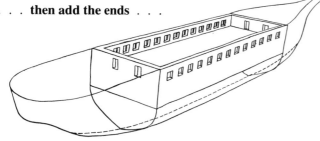

The long box of the citadel had to be given a bow, a stern and underwater shape. The citadel could now float, be stable as a gun platform and have speed through the water. The parts that formed the ship-shape were not armoured but made up of wrought iron plates only ½–1 inch thick; since they could be pierced easily by enemy shot it was made a feature of the design that if the ends were shattered and flooded the central citadel would still float. To reduce the effects of holing even further, the fore and aft sections were subdivided into many watertight compartments. The shape of the whole owed much to the ideas of John Scott Russell, and with a draught of 26–7 feet and a length of 380 feet the hull form had the look of a fast clipper ship.

. . . and now make it move.

There was little in *Warrior*'s sail plan and engine layout that was new, and the official specification simply states that she was to have the 'rig of an 80-gun ship of the line'. A speed of nearly 13 knots was expected from the sails alone. Her engines were not of revolutionary design but were the most powerful of her day, and steam at 22 pounds per square inch was expected to give over 14 knots. The important point was that all machinery was to be placed under the citadel with the added protection of wing tanks. In good weather, under sail and full engine power, she was expected to reach 17 knots.

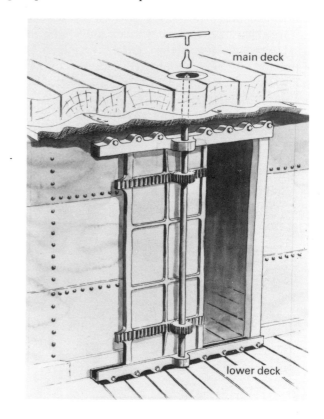

Watertight doors. It is not certain that watertight doors were envisaged at first, but they were certainly added early in the ship's career. They occur at the end of the propeller shaft tunnel where it enters the engine room, and at the openings in the bulkheads on the lower deck within the citadel. Each was operated by a T-bar from the deck above, and when closed jammed hard against a baulk of timber.

Engines and boilers

The engines were made by John Penn and Sons of Greenwich and were jet condensing, horizontal-trunk, single expansion, with a stroke of 4 feet. The bore was 9 feet 4 inches and the piston speed was about 5 m.p.h. giving 55 revolutions per minute. The nominal horse power was stated as 1,250.

Steam was supplied by ten iron, coal-fired boilers, four in the forward boiler room and six in the after room. They were simple fire tube box boilers about 14 feet long, 10 feet wide and 12 feet high, holding about 19 tons of water each (see back cover). As part of the watertight structure, and to support the boilers and engines, *Warrior* had the first double-bottom structure in any naval vessel.

Auxiliary steam

Steam from the boilers was used to drive a large fan which forced air through a network of shafts throughout the ship. In action stations it could be directed to the gun deck alone, where it emerged under pressure between the guns and cleared away the clouds of thick black gun smoke. However this was the only use made of auxiliary steam power, despite the fact that merchant ships were already using steam power to operate winches, windlasses and capstans. Although *Warrior* was to have the heaviest anchors and cables in any Royal Navy vessel to date, the Admiralty made the positive decision that any mechanical aids, such as steam-powered capstans, would disrupt the time-proven methods of seamanship – 'they would spoil the men'.

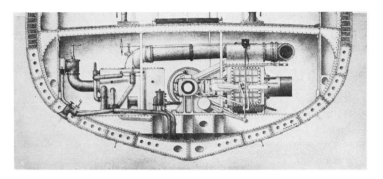

above: *Penn's Horizontal Trunk Engines. This is a contemporary engineer's drawing of a section through the engine room. It is looking aft and the condenser outlets to the sea are on the left, the main cylinders are on the right. Note the double bottom structure and the bilge keels. To the extreme left and right are the wing tanks.*

left: *The engine room of 'Warrior'. Although plans of the engine layout of 'Warrior' are available, there are only two contemporary drawings of her engine room known to exist. One of them is reproduced (left). This was drawn in 1862 when the ship was open to the public and thousands of visitors toured the ship.*

The artist is looking aft along the starboard side of the shaft. The two huge cylinders are to the right, hidden from view. At the top can be seen the large pipe for the exhaust steam, and the gentleman in the top hat has his back to the condenser tank. To the left of the couple on the platform is the small circle of the engine telegraph, and on the far right can be seen the name plate of John Penn and Sons.

Sail power

The main motive power of *Warrior* was her sails and a seaman from the Napoleonic Wars would have been quite at home with her rigging, only the size would have been a surprise. The rigging was that of a normal three-masted warship with each mast made up of three sections: a lower mast, a topmast, and a topgallant. Measuring from the deck up, the dimensions of the main (middle) mast were: lower, 40-inch diameter, 86-foot 3-inch length; topmast, 22-inch diameter, 65-foot length; topgallant, 12½-inch diameter, 52-foot 6-inch length. Allowing for the overlap of each part the total height was about 180 feet. The length of the main yard was 105 feet and she carried a total sail area of 48,400 square feet.

'Up funnel – down screw'

When under sail alone the funnels were lowered so as not to interfere with the sails or cause wind resistance, and the screw was hauled out of the water into the screw well (see pp.3 and 24). When using the engines the order 'Up funnel – down screw' was given. The mainsail was furled and the men on the lower deck turned the winding gear that raised the funnels. At the stern the screw was lowered down the well to lock into the end of the main shaft. To reverse the procedure the order 'Down funnel – up screw' was given.

Mechanism for raising or lowering the screw.
1 'A' frame with lifting tackle. Dismantled when not in use.
2 Hauling parts leading along deck.
3 Locking plate. A seaman had to climb down a ladder inside the well to drop the locking plate; this held the screw in a vertical position.
4 Banjo frame.
5 End of tail-end shaft. It is slotted to receive the bearing shaft of the screw.
6 Cradle supports for banjo frame and screw when lowered.

The propeller and its banjo frame weighed over 35 tons, and had to be raised and lowered by tackles and muscle power alone. Hundreds of seamen had to line the upper deck and haul away. As a safety measure the banjo frame clicked through a series of ratchets as it rose or fell.

Airing the sails.
This sketch from the early 1860s shows 'Warrior' at anchor in fine weather. To take advantage of the light dry wind, the sails have been unfurled and hang loosely to allow them to dry. The royals, topgallants, and the topsails, the three uppermost sails on each mast, are in the lowered position. This picture can be compared with the Dutton print on the front cover, where the sails are in the raised position but the royals have not been set.
The funnels are still in the raised position, the gunport lids are raised and set horizontally and the guns have been run out. The hammocks are stowed neatly in the hammock rack along the top of the upper deck bulwark, and in this picture they appear as a row of white humps.

The armour

Warrior's armour completely enclosed the citadel and was designed to resist any known shot. The ends of the citadel had 4-inch wrought iron plates backed by 12 inches of teak. At the sides the plates were 4½ inches thick, 15 feet by 3 feet and weighing 4 tons each, all interlocked by tonguing and grooving. Each gun port was strengthened by an additional 4-inch plate. The whole side armour was backed by 18 inches of teak made up of a 10-inch horizontal layer and an 8-inch vertical one. The whole was bolted onto the skin of the ship which was set back to receive the armour. The teak acted as a cushion against shot and was considered to equal about 3 inches of iron plate. No consideration was given to armouring the upper deck and since the armour only extended 6 feet below the waterline no thought had been given to mines or torpedoes. The American Civil War of 1861–5 first showed that these weapons were a serious threat. In 1860 *Warrior* was considered to be an impregnable floating fortress

'Warrior's' side armour. Shipbuilder's model now in Science Museum, London.

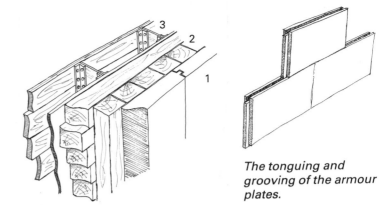

The tonguing and grooving of the armour plates.

1 *Wrought iron plates on the outside.*
2 *The two layers of teak.*
3 *The frames of the ship clad with 2 inches of wood.*

Rifle-proof conning tower

If *Warrior* had lain alongside an enemy in close action, the officers conning the ship on an expanse of almost empty upper deck would have been very vulnerable, especially now that rifles were very accurate over long ranges. The Admiralty solution was to build a small oval tower on the deck (*Gloire* also had one). Just over man height, it was made of teak 12 inches thick, covered by 3-inch plates of iron. Loopholes allowed the officers to view the decks and sails, and a hole at their feet communicated to helmsmen below. Although scorned by 'old style' officers the little tower was a pointer to the future development of centralised control.

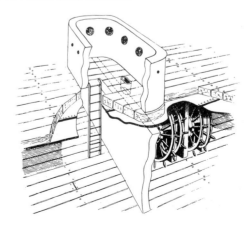

The great guns

The limited strength of wood imposed a maximum on the size of the guns that a wooden warship could carry. To prevent stress they had a large number of relatively small guns spread throughout their decks. Most of the broadside guns of ships in the 1850s were 32-pounders (a gun that fired a shot weighing 32 pounds). *Warrior*'s iron structure enabled her to carry twenty-six 68-pounders and ten 100-pounders. Her broadside of thirteen 68-pounders and six 100-pounders (two 100-pounders could fire either side) threw a weight of 1,484 pounds at her foe. Since a 100-gun wooden ship could throw about 1,600 pounds, this did not seem to the uninformed public to be an improvement. The experts pointed out that one 68-pound shot had the destructive power of five 32-pound shot and one 100-pound shot that of seven, so in reality *Warrior* had the power of 3,500 pounds fired from smaller guns. The public were suitably impressed; and so were the French.

Smooth-bore muzzle-loaders

The standard type of naval gun was the smooth-bore muzzle-loader, basically unchanged in hundreds of years, simple, reliable and logical to use. Its drawback was that it could not increase its power without considerably increasing its size. Double shotting (loading two cannon balls) only reduced power and the two shot soon diverged making aiming impossible. Heavier elongated shot tumbled and swung in flight. It was agreed that unless a smooth-bore gun was increased in size there was no way of increasing its punch.

The appearance of *Warrior* opened the way for the fitting of very heavy guns on ships and her massive main armament was such a dramatic advance that the four 40-pounders carried on her upper deck seemed almost trivial.

Ranges of a 68-pounder smooth-bore muzzle-loader firing solid shot with a 16-pound powder charge.

ELEVATION	½°	1°	3°	6°	10°	15°
RANGE (yards)	340	640	1,400	2,180	2,880	3,620
TIME OF FLIGHT (sec)	½	1½	4	7	11	15

Muzzle velocity was 1,280 ft/sec and 3,000 yards was considered the limit of accuracy.

In ricochet firing (where the shot skimmed the water) an elevation of ¼° sent the shot about 300 yards, then it continued skimming for 32 grazes until at 2,900 yards it diverged off target. Its velocity was of course considerably reduced.

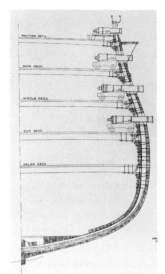
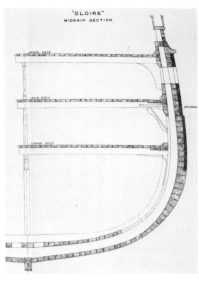

above left: *Section through HMS 'Marlborough', the flagship in the Mediterranean in 1860, a screw-driven first-rate ship of the line, wooden and unarmoured, carrying 131 guns on three decks, most of them 32-pounders. She was 245 feet long, could reach nearly 12 knots and was considered one of the finest warships afloat.*

above right: *Section through 'Gloire' showing that she was a wooden ship with iron plates bolted onto her hull, and had one main deck for her guns.*

below: *Section through the main gun deck of 'Warrior', the ship that could outsail, outgun and pulverise 'Marlborough' while remaining unscathed. Both types of gun are shown: to the right is a 68-pounder smooth-bore muzzle-loader (see opposite page) and left is a 100-pounder breech-loader (p. 14). Note the raised gunport lids; they were made of thin sheets of iron, bullet-proof only, and each had a small viewing port in its centre.*

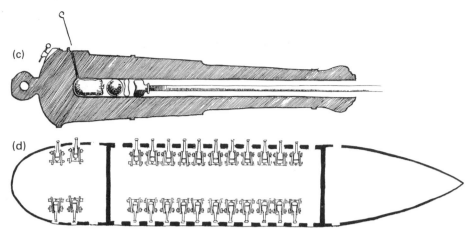

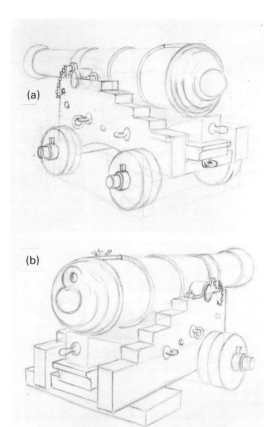

(a) Wheel (truck) carriage. Tackles (ropes and blocks) were hooked to the carriage and the ship's side to manoeuvre for firing and to help absorb the recoil. The gun was elevated by means of a wedge (quoin) thrust beneath the breech.

(b) Rear chock carriage. To help reduce the recoil of heavier guns, the rear wheels of the standard carriage were replaced by a large chock of timber. This device was introduced in the Napoleonic Wars and had become commonplace by the 1850s.

(c) Section through 68-pounder. This section shows the cartridge at the rear of the bore, followed by the shot and wad, then the ramrod. A cartridge pricker is positioned above the vent hole.

Overall length 11 feet 3 inches; greatest width 2 feet 3.76 inches; width at muzzle 18.65 inches; bore 8.12 inches.

(d) Positions of 68-pounders on main deck of 'Warrior'.

A 68-pounder smooth-bore muzzle-loader

Slide and rear chock on 'Warrior'. Both wheel (truck) and rear chock carriages needed wide gunports, about 4 feet wide, to enable the guns to slew left or right. 'Warrior' was originally designed with such ports but before her completion it was decided to mount the carriages on pivots. The slide was pivoted at the ship's side so it was possible to reduce the width of the gunports to 2 feet and still retain the slew angles of about 30° each side. The old style tackles were still used but friction tubes fired by a lanyard had replaced the flintlock mechanism.

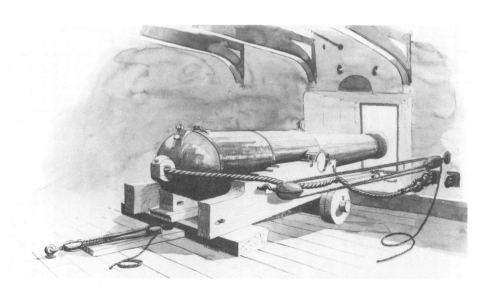

Rifled breech-loaders

Rifling and breech loading were not new ideas but industrial technology had been unable to overcome manufacturing difficulties until the 1850s when William Armstrong successfully introduced small calibre rifled guns that could be loaded at the breech. *Warrior* was supplied with his latest design firing shot of 100 pounds, later increased to 110 pounds.

Rifled guns could fire elongated shot, heavier than round shot of the same bore, and with much greater accuracy. The rifling bit into the lead coating of the shot as it passed along the barrel. This made the shot spin, kept it steady in flight, and the tapered point struck the target first.

Breech-loading guns did not have to be withdrawn inboard to be loaded and they promised to make firing quicker, and more accurate. Unfortunately, it turned out that the breeching mechanism was not sufficiently strong and safe for guns of this size, and they were withdrawn after a few years. For the next twenty years the Admiralty concentrated on muzzle-loading guns, both smooth-bore and rifled.

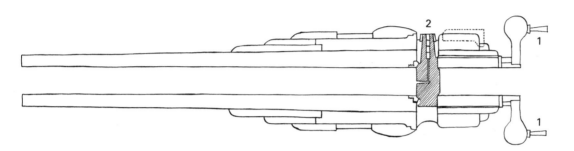

left: *Section of Armstrong gun.*
1 *Handles to unscrew the breech piece.*
2 *Vent piece.*
The barrel is reinforced by strengthening bands.

below: *Position of 100-pounders on 'Warrior'.*

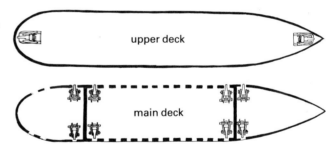

upper deck

main deck

The Armstrong 100-pounder

Eight of these 100-pounder rifled breech-loaders were on the main deck of 'Warrior', on carriages very similar to those for the 68-pounders. Two 100-pounders were on the upper deck on slides that could be swung to fire either side of the vessel. Racers were set in the deck to guide the slides.

The two handles at the rear of the gun were turned to unscrew the inner piece and allow it to move back about 1 inch. This released pressure on the movable vent piece, which could then be lifted out of the gun; the handles to lift the vent piece can be seen in the drawing. The shell and cartridge could now be pushed into the breech, the vent piece replaced, and the handles tightened to hold the vent firmly in position. The gun was fired in the same way as the 68-pounder.

Other guns

The upper deck of *Warrior* carried four 40-pounders (Armstrong breech-loaders) which, along with the twenty-six 68-pounders and ten 100-pounders gave her a classification as a 40-gun ship.

Not counted in the classification were two 25-pounders, a 12-pounder and a 6-pounder. One of the 25-pounders was a field piece and had a standard land carriage and caisson for use ashore.

Although the arrangement of her armament retained the broadside concept of the past, the size and structure of the guns themselves suggested the revolutionary potential of iron warships. By the 1870s 30-ton guns were in use at sea.

Shot and shell

Round shot

Solid balls of metal were the basic projectiles for all smooth-bore muzzle-loaders. They could be made of wrought iron, chilled iron, cast iron or steel, and, since they all had to have the same diameter, '68-pound round shot' could in fact vary in weight from 67 to 72 pounds. The diameter of every 68-pound shot was 7.92 inches to fit the bore of 8.12 inches. The gap of 0.2 inch (0.1 inch each side of the shot) was called windage and allowed the shot to be loaded easily, yet it did not allow much of the explosive gases to escape on firing. The shot were painted and stowed in racks around the gun deck, which

meant that they had to be carefully checked for rust or thick paint before loading.

Round shells

These were hollow metal spheres of 7.92-inch diameter weighing 47 pounds and could be filled with powder to give a total weight of nearly 61 pounds. A metal or wooden fuse with a combustible centre filling was screwed into the shell. It was ignited by the firing of the gun and the length of the fuse governed the time before the shell exploded, the intention being that it should explode a fraction of a second after hitting the target. In the past shells had been unreliable, but they were now improving; as early as the 1820s the French artillery expert Paixhans was urging that French warships be armed almost exclusively with shells.

Elongated shot and shell

On *Warrior* elongated shot or shells were used in the rifled breech-loaders only, and had a coating of lead which took up the rifling of the barrel. They were 16 inches long and 7 inches in diameter to fit the bore exactly. The elongated shell could have a time fuse, as in the round shell, but, since it kept its point forward all the way to the target, it could be fitted with a percussion fuse in its nose so as to explode on impact.

For use at close quarters against enemy crews, both muzzle-loaders and breech-loaders had a supply of case shot, and the breech-loaders had special segmented shells designed to burst into fragments.

Round shells. Whole and in section. The wooden base fastened to the shell was to ensure that when loaded in the barrel the fuse was always pointing outwards. If the shell turned in the barrel, the fuse would be immediately forced into the shell when the gun was fired, and the whole would explode inside the barrel.

Boxer's 7½ second time fuse. Whole and in section. The protective cap was unscrewed before the shell was rammed down the gun barrel. When ignited by the explosion in the gun barrel the central combustible material burnt down for 7½ seconds until it reached the clear hole at the bottom where it ignited the bursting charge in the shell. A reduction in the time was obtained by boring out the sealing material in the appropriate hole above.

Wooden fuses, similar in construction, were still in use but were slowly being replaced by brass fuses. There were two types in use in the navy, each named after its inventor – Boxer's fuses and Moorsom's fuses.

3 The first black battleship

The building of *Warrior*

On 25 May 1859, six months before *Gloire* was launched, work started on *Warrior* at the Thames Iron Works, Blackwall. The iron beams were subcontracted to the Butterley Iron Company of Derbyshire. Throughout 1859 and 1860 thousands of workers teamed like ants around the growing shape. The noise was described as earsplitting, but some said the chatter of thousands of interested bystanders drowned the noise of the work.

Considering the revolutionary nature of *Warrior* and constant alterations by the Admiralty it was no surprise that the eleven month deadline could not be met. However, the Admiralty waived the penalty clause and added to the contract price. Nineteen months after the laying of the keel *Warrior* was ready for launching.

The day chosen for the launching was 29 December 1860, the time 2.30 p.m., and Sir John Pakington, who had been First Lord of the Admiralty when *Warrior* was ordered, was to launch her. The icy weather threatened to freeze the hull to the slipway but workmen manned huge screws and levered her forward. Slowly she began to creep towards the water and as she gathered speed Sir John smashed a bottle of wine on the moving bow and said 'God speed the *Warrior*!' It was 3.00 p.m. *Gloire* had been commissioned for four months.

Warrior was moved to Victoria dock and then to Greenhithe, and on 19 September she sailed for Spithead. After sea trials she was handed over to the government on 24 October 1861. *Gloire*, after fourteen months of fame, was no longer a threat to Britain.

Lining the shore, the public watched her trials and compared her with the familiar high-sided and striped wooden battleships they knew so well. This was a new type of ship, massive but long, low, black and threatening. It was here that a phrase was heard that was to follow her all her career: 'She looks like a black snake amongst the rabbits.'

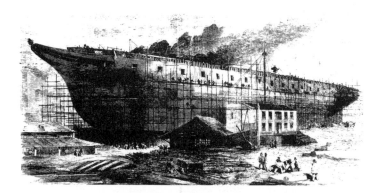

right above: *'Warrior' nearing completion, late 1860. The armour plates are not yet in position. Notice the lack of large cranes. Most of the lifting of heavy material was by sheerlegs or derricks built onto the upper deck.*

'Warrior' was constantly being featured in the press. Comments ranged from patriotic fervour to doubts that she would ever float. Her high cost, £379,154, excluding armour, caused much debate; this was more than double the cost of a wooden three decker – 'Marlborough' cost £176,300.

right below: *The main (or gun) deck under construction 1860.*
This is the view from the after bulkhead of the citadel, looking forward on the port side. On the deck, forward of the capstan, is the skylight to the lower deck and engine room. On the left the gunports stretch away and planking is ready for laying on the iron plates of the deck. Most of the decks and bulkheads in 'Warrior' are clad with timber.
There was a long way to go before fitting the gun carriages so the carriage was probably just an improvised wheelbarrow.

The pride of Britain

Being so new and innovatory *Warrior* needed many minor adjustments, and was not really considered ready for action until June 1862. However, as far as the world was concerned she was a force to be reckoned with from late 1861. So obviously superior to anything in existence she had no need to prove herself. Even her worst detractors had to admit that she could tackle whole fleets of wooden ships with impunity. No enemy dared challenge her. French dreams of revenge and glory at sea faded away. Britain settled back with a feeling of security and self-satisfaction. Only a few far-seeing individuals analysed with foreboding the implications of the creation of *Warrior*.

On display

Warrior joined the Channel Squadron for her first commission which lasted until November 1864, and she sailed north European waters with the occasional trip to Lisbon and Gibraltar. She was greeted as the wonder of the age and ambassadors from many nations inspected her. The royalty of Europe walked her decks, but Queen Victoria never came to see her; Prince Albert had died in the December of 1861 and the Queen had gone into mourning.

    Warrior toured British ports and the public flocked aboard in their thousands. She was truly the Pride of Britain.

right above: *Although this photograph was taken in the early 1870s, there had been little change to 'Warrior's' appearance since she was built. As part of her drydocking work her jib and flying jib have been removed, her royal and topgallant yards have been lowered to the decks and her topgallant masts are half lowered. Note her black hull, with only a thin white line at the waterline and a thicker one along her upper bulwarks and hammock racks. This photograph, with the network of masts, yards and rigging so obvious, shows that, despite her engines, she is constructed as a sailing ship.*

right below: *'Beggar my Neighbour'. This 'Punch' cartoon of 1861 reflects the popular feelings of delight at the squashing of the French dreams of sea superiority. Napoleon III's card 'Gloire' is taken by Britain's card 'Warrior', played by Palmerston. The French Emperor has a bag of francs beside his chair, but the British prime minister has an equally large bag of sovereigns, worth far more. Palmerston's attitude and expression convey a feeling of easy superiority.*

The black snake

This wooden wall ran round the whole upper deck, and, except as indicated in the sketch, it was topped by a hammock rack. Hammocks were stowed here when not in use, and were covered by a canvas topping.

The upper deck

To simplify the layout all small fittings such as pin rails, sheep pens, flag lockers etc. have been omitted. The large boats, shrouds and davits are not shown on the starboard side.

The upper deck is iron plated and covered with wood planking 4 inches thick and 8 inches wide.

1 Stern pivot gun (100-pounder breech-loader)
2 Captain's skylight
3 Ladder down to officers' quarters
4 Mizzen mast
5 Main compass, steering wheels, and steering compasses
6 Rifle-proof conning tower
7 After bridge, with engine telegraphs
8 Capstan
9 Main mast
10 Ship's boats (also three on starboard side)

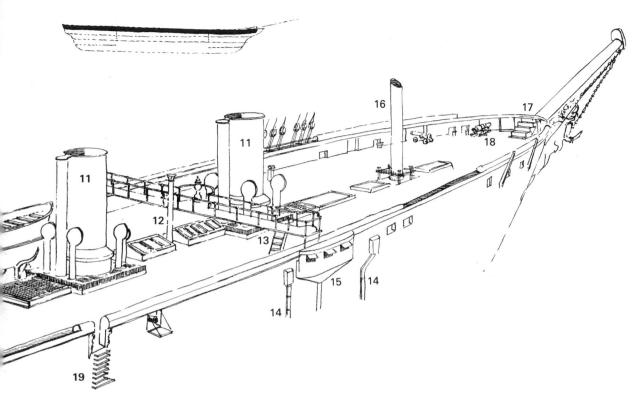

Stern view
At the waterline can be seen the lower opening of the screw well. The captain's gig is partially lowered. At either side the wooden boom davits are shown in the raised and lowered positions (starboard and port respectively).

11 Telescopic funnels
12 Galley funnel
13 Forward bridge
14 Ash shoots
15 Latrines
16 Foremast
17 Steps leading over bulwarks to latrines (heads) and bowsprit
18 Bow pivot gun (100-pounder breech-loader)
19 Entry port and ladderway

Main deck *(simplified)*
1 *Screw well*
2 *Yoke tillers*
3 *Captain's cabins*
4 *Master's cabin*
5 *Commander's cabin*
6 *Mooring bitts and Downton pump*
7 *Latrines (officers only)*
8 *Main deck steering wheels and steering compasses*
9 *A 68-pounder muzzle-loader gun*
10 *Mess table and benches*
N.B. *every gun bay would have been fully equipped like this one.*

11 *Hawse pipes (Spurling gates) to chain locker below*
12 *Water tank*
13 *Secondary capstan*
14 *Funnel casings*
15 *Galley*
16 *A 100-pounder breech-loader gun*
17 *Water tanks*
18 *Latrines*
19 *Mooring bitts*
20 *Bowsprit stepped onto large timber*
21 *Bowsprit*

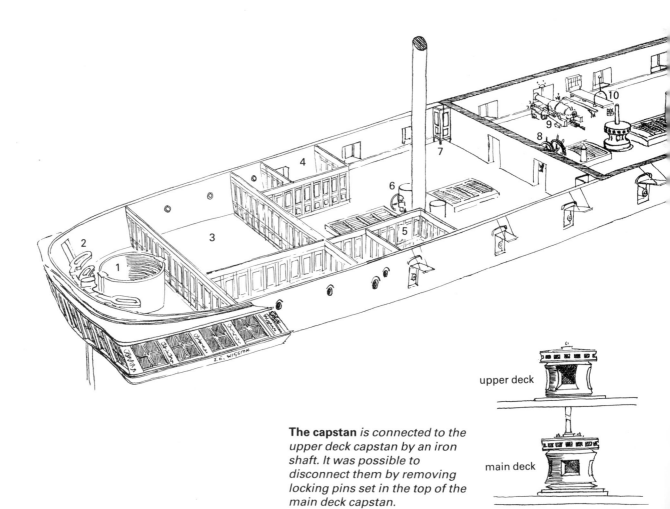

The capstan *is connected to the upper deck capstan by an iron shaft. It was possible to disconnect them by removing locking pins set in the top of the main deck capstan.*

upper deck

main deck

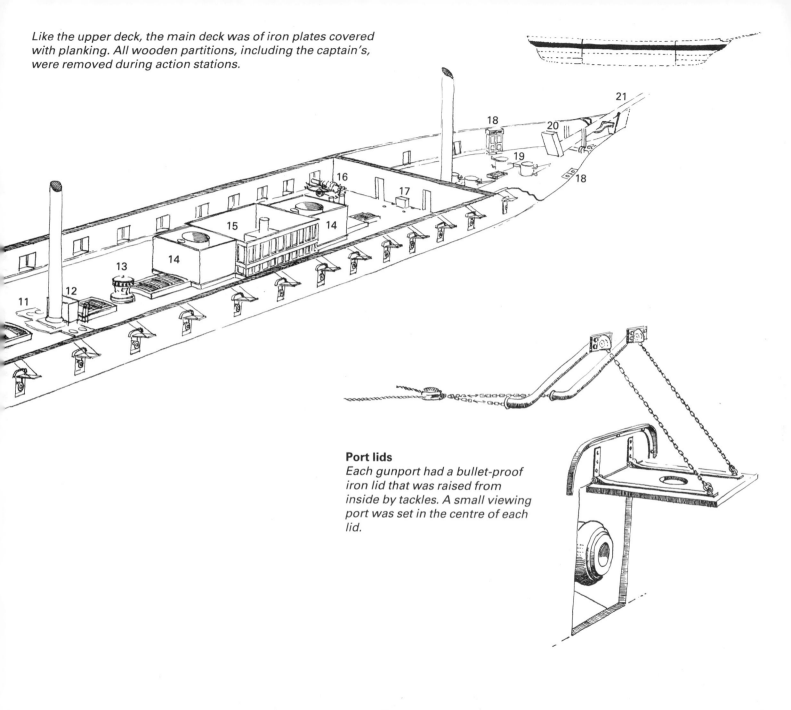

Like the upper deck, the main deck was of iron plates covered
with planking. All wooden partitions, including the captain's,
were removed during action stations.

Port lids
Each gunport had a bullet-proof
iron lid that was raised from
inside by tackles. A small viewing
port was set in the centre of each
lid.

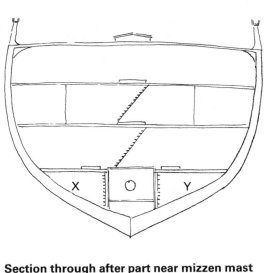

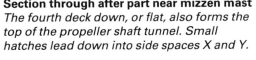

The lower deck and flats *(simplified)*
1 Captain's storeroom
2 Wardroom and officers' cabins
3 Gunroom
4 Hand-up areas for after magazine
5 Standby steering wheels
6 Wing tanks (run the full length of citadel on each side)
7 Hatch to bread room; hatch to engine room. Dispensary; band instruments store; chronometer and compass room. Bag racks for seamen at sides.
8 Downton pump
9 Entrances to cable lockers, shot lockers and shell rooms below; vertical tubes are ventilating pipes leading to main deck above
10 After funnel casing with bag racks on each side
11 Forward funnel casing
12 Engineers' berth and hand-up areas for forward magazine

Section through after part near mizzen mast
The fourth deck down, or flat, also forms the top of the propeller shaft tunnel. Small hatches lead down into side spaces X and Y.

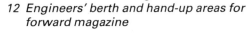

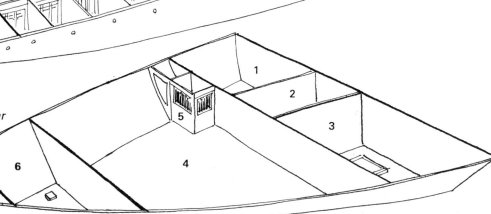

After hold, or flat
1 Store for pork, pease, sugar and vinegar
2 Store for candles, tea, chocolate, raisins and lime juice
3 Store for beef, flour, tobacco and soap
4 Chest room
5 Engineers' storeroom
6 Wardroom mess store

13 Sailroom, cable store and prisons
14 Boatswain's, gunner's and carpenter's berths; engineers' messroom
15 Sick berth   16 Gunroom stores
17 Plug ports (tubes through wing tanks to let in light: in rough weather they were sealed by a wooden plug on the end of an iron bar)

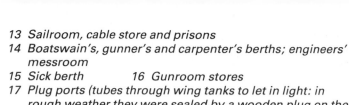

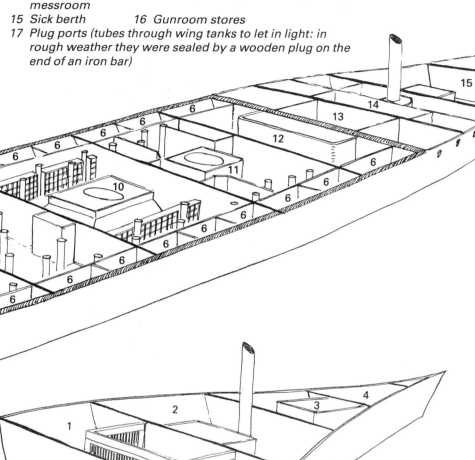

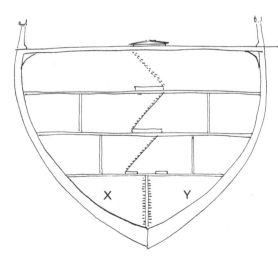

Fore hold, or flat
1 Rope stores, sail stores and drying room (the drying room was on the port side, with a special stove warming the air)
2 Boatswain's and carpenter's stores
3 Spare sails and small rope store
4 Blocks, tackles, belaying pins etc.; rocket gear

Section through forward part near foremast
There is no propeller shaft forward, so below the flat the lower hold is divided, X and Y, by a single fore and aft bulkhead.

Warrior was a curious mixture of the traditional and the new. Scott Russell had even said 'Jack likes a pretty figurehead to his ships and I do not see why we should knock it off.' An emotional reaction to the new elements in the ship came from Admiral Sir Edward Belcher who described her as 'This miserable, pegtopped, leangutted model!' Such a man was living in the glorious past; it was the young officers who sailed *Warrior* who were to understand and develop the potentials built into her.

Cut-away view
(simplified, to illustrate points not possible to show on deck sketches)
1 The 'A' frame, for lifting the propeller, in position
2 Propeller shaft and tunnel
3 After magazine – in two sections astride the tunnel
4 Bread room; stretches across the ship, and from lower deck to ship's bottom; used to store ship's biscuits
5 Engine room; sketch shows starboard side condenser with intake and outlet pipes to circulate cooling sea water
6 Chain lockers, shot lockers and shell rooms
7 Bunkers
8 Railway lines and coal truck in each bunker
9 Casing around smoke uptakes from boilers
10 Boilers
11 Forward magazine
12 Cathead and anchor

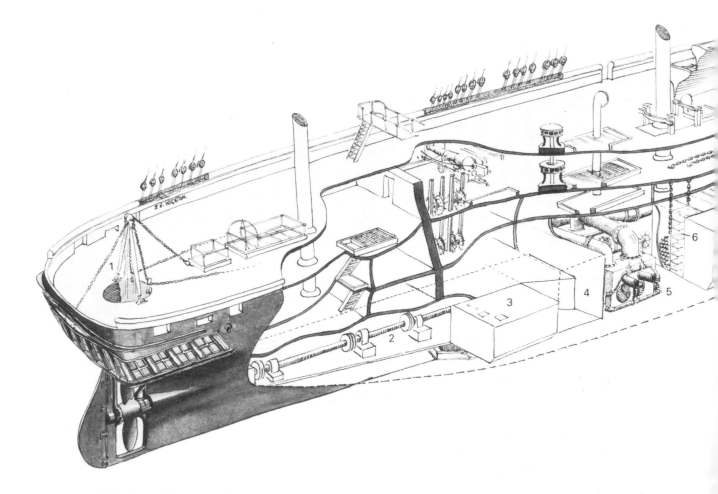

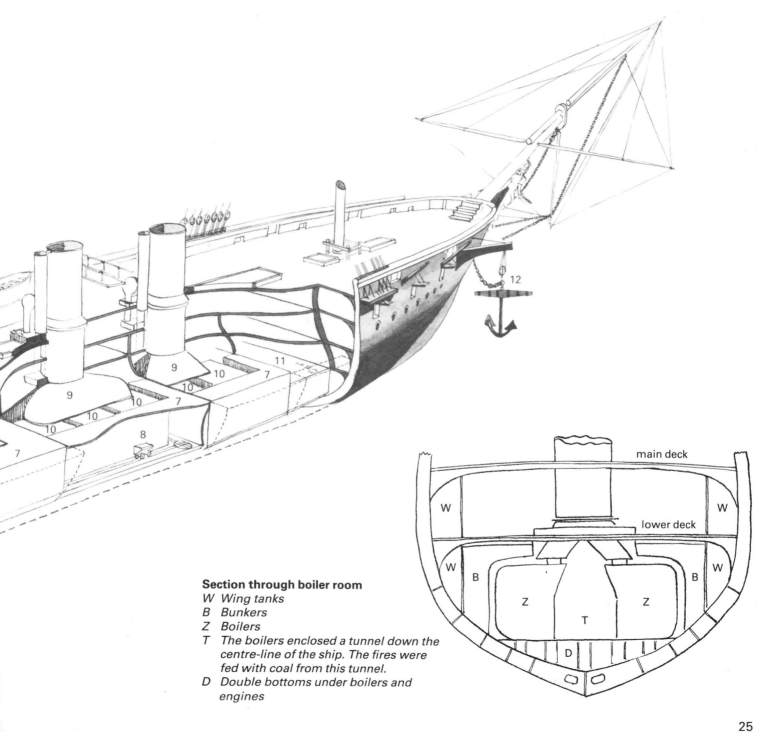

Section through boiler room

W Wing tanks

B Bunkers

Z Boilers

T The boilers enclosed a tunnel down the centre-line of the ship. The fires were fed with coal from this tunnel.

D Double bottoms under boilers and engines

main deck

lower deck

Living conditions

Although she was the most powerful warship afloat, *Warrior*, with her single main gun deck and armament of 40 guns, was, according to the unbending Admiralty regulations, a fifth-rate frigate, much to the annoyance and confusion of naval officers who still considered a frigate to be a small fast scouting ship not strong enough to take her place in a line of battle. A frigate should have had a compliment of 300 but finally *Warrior*'s manning was decided as about 700:

42 deck officers, 3 warrant officers and 445 seamen;

3 marine officers, 6 N.C.O.s and 118 marine artillery;

2 chief engineers, 10 engineers and 66 stokers and trimmers.

Instead of being press-ganged or signing on for an unspecified length of time, sailors now enjoyed a new career structure that had come into being in 1853. Jack Tar, still often called 'Poor Jack', now signed on for a fixed engagement, took an oath of loyalty and could look forward to either signing on again or accepting a pension. Jack now wore a standard uniform, was better educated and better looked after – though flogging was not suspended until 1880.

For the officers life was more comfortable, but long periods of peace did nothing to help their careers. Promotion became very slow and the navy had some very old lieutenants, while others retired early.

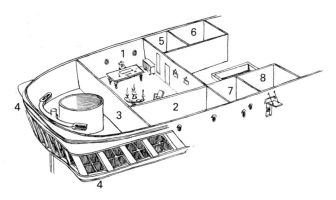

Senior officers' accommodation

1 Captain's day room	5 Pantry for captain's steward
2 Captain's bedroom	6 Master's cabin
3 Captain's after cabins	7 Office
4 Captain's latrine	8 Commander's cabin

The captain's cabin was the only cabin which was lit and ventilated from above, and his door, and the area forward of the three cabins, was guarded by marine sentries. No one approached unless he had official reasons for so doing.

The captain's 'clutter'.

No photographs are available of the furniture and fittings of 'Warrior's' interior. Much evidence exists to show that the captain made himself at home, filling his rooms with personal furniture and belongings. This photograph is probably from the early 1870s and shows the captain's cabin on 'Bellerophon'; 'Warrior's' would have been very similar. It looks rather like a typical Victorian drawing room, and only the beams overhead show clearly that it is aboard a ship. All this, including the cabin partitions, would have been hurriedly passed below during action stations.

Note the stove. Several of this type were found on 'Warrior' though none is shown on the plans. It suggests that the officers had the freedom to make such additions.

This is one of the only three known photographs of the upper deck of 'Warrior'. The date of the photograph is late 1869 or early 1870.

The figure standing centre is the captain and behind him, in his mortar board and gown, is the chaplain (also naval instructor). The figure far left with the pill box hat is probably the captain of marine artillery. In 1862 the chaplain received 5s 9d per day, the captain of marine artillery 12s 1d per day.

Lieutenants were paid about 10s 0d per day and the young gunnery lieutenant appointed in March 1863 was John Arbuthnot Fisher ('Jackie' Fisher) who became Admiral of the Fleet Lord Fisher and was instrumental in the introduction of the new Dreadnought battleships forty years later.

Senior officers' quarters

The captain was in complete command of the vessel. He lived in isolation, in spacious accommodation at the after end of the vessel.

The commander was second in command to the captain, with a cabin on the starboard side aft.

The master was in charge of the sailing of the ship and its navigation. His cabin was opposite the commander's on the port side.

All these cabins were considered part of the gun deck, and the master and commander each shared his cabin with a 68-pounder gun. On the call to action stations the partitions of all these cabins and their furniture were cleared away.

Signing on the ship in August 1861 were:

Captain	Hon. Arthur A. Cochrane	Daily pay £1 0s 0d
Commander	George Tryon	Daily pay £0 16s 6d
Master	George H. Blakey	Daily pay £0 13s 0d

The wardroom

With the exception of the most junior (the sub-lieutenants and midshipmen) the officers were berthed on the lower deck, beneath the commander's and master's cabins. Fourteen cabins were ranged along the ship's side, seven to port and seven to starboard, all connected by sliding doors to the central eating and relaxing area known as the wardroom.

Each cabin measured about 6 feet by 10 feet and held a bunk, a collapsable table, and a washstand complete with basin and water jug; anything else the occupant had to supply from his own pocket. A little light came in through the high-placed small scuttle; but without the use of candles and oil lamps the cabins would have been dark and gloomy.

By contrast, the wardroom was lit by a large skylight which was placed beneath a similar skylight on the upper deck, so under certain circumstances it was possible to have sunlight streaming in. Right aft was a general purpose pantry, kitchen and crockery store for use by the stewards who served the officers. Centrally, beneath the skylight, stood a huge table, ringed with chairs, where the officers took their meals. Abiding by a tradition stretching back hundreds of years, the wardroom table was cleared during action stations and used as an operating table by the surgeon. The officers turned the wardroom into a comfortable relaxing area by installing carpets, small tables, armchairs, mirrors, potted plants and a piano.

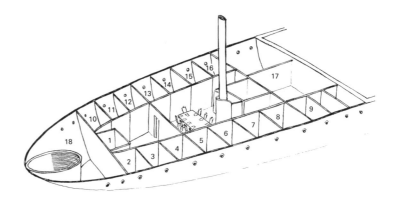

The wardroom
(The names of the first officers to serve in 'Warrior' are shown.)
1 Pantry for wardroom stewards
2 Assistant surgeon's cabin – William J. Asslin
3 2nd chief engineer – William Glasspole
4 Surgeon – Samuel S.D. Wells
5 1st lieutenant – Henry B. Phillimore
6 2nd lieutenant – Joseph E.M. Wilson
7 5th lieutenant – Noel S.F. Digby
8 1st chief engineer – William Buchan
9 Assistant surgeon – Edmund W. Coleman M.D. (note that he is berthed in the gunroom – not the wardroom)
10 2nd lieutenant of marine artillery – Francis H.E. Owen
11 1st lieutenant of marine artillery – Herbert Everitt
12 Chaplain and naval instructor – Revd Robert N. Jackson
13 Captain of marine artillery – Henry W. Mawbey
14 4th lieutenant – Henry L. Perceval
15 3rd lieutenant – George F.H. Parker
16 Paymaster – John N. De Vries
17 Gunroom
18 Captain's storeroom

left: *A typical gunroom. No photograph exists of 'Warrior's' gunroom but this one, taken in 1899 on 'Repulse', gives a general impression. The large table served as a mess, study and general purpose table.*

This is a specially posed photograph suggesting a quiet studious atmosphere. On 'Warrior' the gunroom held over twenty boisterous sub-lieutenants and midshipmen, suggesting a noisy, bustling area.

The gunroom and chestroom

Forward of the wardroom lay the gunroom, home of the midshipmen and sub-lieutenants. On the starboard side it held an assistant surgeon's cabin, an office and a pantry. On the port side was the messroom, a dark cavern-like area, lit by three small scuttles. The central section was lit by the skylight above, and on the deck three hatches led down to store rooms. Around the bulkheads were ranged rows of drawer units and washstands.

Since 20 to 30 lively and vocal boys washed, changed, ate, studied and relaxed here it must have been the noisiest part of the ship. There were no fitments for hammocks so the youngsters had to sleep on collapsable beds or, with permission, hang hammocks elsewhere.

There was no room for the sea chests containing their personal effects; these had to be stowed in the chestroom. To reach their sea chests they had to climb up to the main deck, then down to the wardroom level (where the officers must have been thankful that the ladder was partitioned off!), and then down to the chestroom. In this dark cave, lit only by candles or lamps, their chests were laid in rows along with water tanks, spare shot and large hawsers – but for a while they could open their sea chests and live in a private world.

Joining *Warrior* in 1861 was a midshipman, the fourteen year old Henry Arthur Keith Murray. Going about his normal duties he could not guess that over 120 years later his name was to be used constantly and gratefully by historical researchers (p.47).

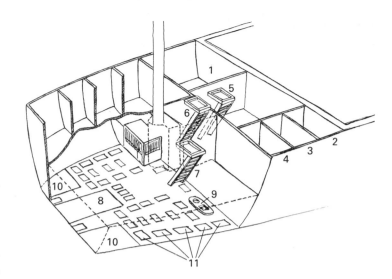

Gunroom and chestroom
1. *Gunroom: midshipmen's mess*
2. *Gunroom pantry*
3. *Office*
4. *Assistant surgeon's cabin*
5. *Ladder up from gunroom to main deck*
6. *Ladder down from main deck to wardroom: this was partitioned off from the wardroom*
7. *Ladder from wardroom down to chestroom*
8. *18-inch hawsers stowed here*
9. *Spare cap for main mast*
10. *Spare water tanks stowed here*
11. *Over 30 sea chests belonging to the midshipmen and sub-lieutenants were arranged in rows on the deck of the chestroom.*

Writing home – a middy and his sea chest. The crowded and active conditions of the gunroom precluded moments of quiet privacy. But in the depths of the chestroom, among his own belongings and souvenirs of home, a midshipman could enter his own private world. No photographs of below decks in 'Warrior' exist, and this photograph, taken about 25 years later and on a different ship, must serve to illustrate the scene. It shows the normal rows of chests and a boy writing home: the inside of the chest lid is covered with photographs of his family.

Warrior's crew

The three important warrant officers, the boatswain, the carpenter and gunner, each had a cabin alongside the engineers' messroom in the fore part of the lower deck (p.23). The ten engineers and assistant engineers also berthed on the lower deck, just forward of the boiler rooms and above the forward magazine (p.23).

The rest of the crew, the petty officers, seamen, stokers, marine artillery and boys, well over 600 men, slept and ate between the guns on the main deck; most of them within the walls of the citadel. Long mess tables were positioned between the guns, and the original plans of *Warrior* show a total of 34 tables, 28 within and 6 outside the citadel. This gives about 18 men per table. On the bulkhead against the ship's side, above the table, a crockery rack held a basin, plate and spoon for each man in the mess. Set in the beams overhead were strong hooks, 24½ inches apart, for slinging hammocks. Most of the crew's belongings were stowed in banks of bag racks on the lower deck, but small ditty bags or boxes were allowed at the mess tables. 'Poor Jack' is said to have 'loved a fugg' and distrusted fresh air, so he kept the gunport lids

above: *This sketch (about 1858) was reflecting the proud and clean-cut image that the British public had of its navy. The knife on the lanyard was an indispensable working tool, but it was also the only knife available for the seaman to cut his meat with at mealtimes. The young boy represents a powderman: by his side can be seen a leather cartridge case, and the object under his arm may be another.*

left: *'Night alarm'. This lively and imaginative sketch from the 1860s takes a humorous view of the scene when the crew have been suddenly called to action stations, but it is full of accurate detail.*
  Note that this is a wooden ship – the beams and deckhead are wood, unlike 'Warrior's'. Clearly visible are the cartridge cases under the arms of the seamen in the foreground, and so are the numbers on the gun and a hammock. The bugler is a marine, as is the man on the right with his arm outstretched.

closed as much as possible. The gun deck must have been a dream to him, with its close-packed humanity, men singing, talking, playing cards and attempting to write letters home. Many had musical instruments, others had pet cats, dogs, monkeys, canaries and parrots. Large wooden spittoons were placed at intervals for the benefit of the tobacco chewers. Normally smoking was limited to the upper deck. Officers, usually smoking cigarettes, to one side, the seamen, usually smoking pipes, to the other. Sometimes smoking around a lantern was allowed on the gun deck.

Rate of wages in the Royal Navy c.1860

RATING	PER MONTH OF 31 DAYS			PER YEAR		
	£	s.	d.	£	s.	d.
Chief petty officers	3	9	9	41	1	3
First-class working petty officers	3	2	0	36	10	0
Second-class working petty officers	2	16	10	33	9	2
Leading seamen	2	14	3	31	18	9
Able seamen	2	9	1	28	17	11
Ordinary seamen	1	18	9	22	16	3
Second-class ordinary seamen	1	11	0	18	5	0
Boys (first-class), and naval apprentices	0	18	1	10	12	11
Boys of the second class	0	15	6	9	2	6

Seamen-gunners, who are men trained in the *Excellent*, receive 4d per day in the first class, and 2d per day in the second class, in addition to all other pay of their ratings. Also five years' service are allowed to be counted as six, for a pension.

A visit to *Warrior*

The following eyewitness description of life aboard *Warrior* includes the scene on the gun deck, September 1863. The seamen are on their best behaviour, presenting an image of the British tar that obviously impressed the visitor.

'Visitors are received on board with the greatest courtesy, and every one on board vies with each other to give information. Several officers were going about with ladies and gentlemen, explaining the working of the Armstrong guns; and it was amusing to see the interest taken by ladies in a subject which might be supposed to be rather unpleasant than otherwise. Along the broad white deck, which looked like a great broad street, men were seen rope making, carpentering, making hammocks, and hand ropes, &c. Sentries were walking their quiet rounds as silently as if there were no crowd around them. Going down the ladder to the main deck, the ear was greeted with the bleating of sheep, and the cackle of domestic fowls in spacious coops, and the animals seemed quite at home among plenty of clean fodder and food. Large quantities of butchers' meat was hanging up ready for cooking. Cooks busy at work in the galley, preparing all sorts of dishes – the smell set up is savoury, and calculated to give one an appetite. It is not yet meat time, yet here and there are seen some of the fine fellows leisurely (it being their watch below, as it is termed) dispatching their "levener", from the hour "eleven" at which it is taken; and which, in one instance, was a goodly snack of fried beefsteaks and onions; and another mutton chops and boiled rice; and in both cases plenty of biscuits. While a great many were eating, many were engaged in reading (Newspapers mostly) or writing letters; some working hearthrugs by a quilting process, or embroidering pictures. Many lay asleep, having to go on deck at twelve o'clock; some sat wrapt in their own meditation, as if unconscious of what was going on around them; one man, a marine, chaunted a song, with a fine cultivated voice; and an artillery-man tried to get up a laugh in his own mess, by pretending to read from a newspaper of a man being drowned by a cart wheel passing over him, but the joke was too stale. It is generally understood on shore that "Jack", when not on duty, is passing round the grog or smoking, but here you found the seamen better occupied in their leisure moments: here was to be seen the quiet family man, who is melted into "softness" by the visit of his dearest female friend, and sits beside her apparently recalling many happy moments, or mending his clothes, or shoes, or doing the barber. We are all familiar with the British seaman as a daring man, and a light-hearted cheery man; we read of him as a hero, and we find him on shore with a soul lifted above all mean and common cares; but we have to visit him in his abode, in order to see him as the homely man. He is a pattern to all the world in the domestic virtues of tidiness, cleanliness, and order: he has, too, no little fancy for the arts; his paintings and sketches have always the touch of nature, while his samplers and needlework would not disgrace the finest and most delicate fingers.'

Food

In port there would be ample supplies of fresh meat and vegetables, but when at sea the ship's own stock of food was used and the best of cooks was hard put to turn out over 700 meals, three times a day on a galley stove 10 feet by 8 feet. Salt pork and salt beef appeared on alternate days and occasionally preserved beef (tinned). Regulations stated that the oldest casks or tins had to be opened first, but the tales that they were eating beef from the Napoleonic War stocks was probably a messdeck myth. However, there were huge stocks of ship's biscuits, usually rock hard and best painted and sent home as a souvenir. Determined and honest attempts to deal with the problem of beetles, moths, meal worms, cockroaches and weevils had failed, and new recruits had to be taught how to deal with the 'fresh meat' in their biscuits.

Salt, pepper, vinegar and plenty of pickles helped the food down, but the best sauce was the daily issue of rum. If the rum ran out then half a pint of wine or a pint of beer was issued. Soups were served daily, and for sweets the cook had to manage with flour, suet, currants or raisins, chocolate and sugar, which tended to limit the variety. Plum duff turned up constantly. Chocolate was a drink regularly supplied, with tea and sometimes coffee as substitutes. No milk was available.

left: *A letter from 'Warrior'. Dated 1878, this letter was written by Charles Alexander to his parents; other letters of that period have a sketch of 'Warrior' as the letterhead. Though typical of the sentimentality so loved by the Victorians, the quotation beneath the drawing is from an earlier writer, Charles Dibdin (1745–1814), whose songs were still popular with seamen. About the time this letter was written, the more lively and humorous songs from Gilbert and Sullivan's 'HMS Pinafore' were also being sung, or whistled, by officers and ratings alike.*

'Dy'e mind the roll she gave?' From the mid 1860s we have this artist's impression of the main deck of a typical warship during a heavy roll. It is rather stiffly drawn, and there are fewer men than would normally be present during a meal, but certain points are worth noting. The guns are in the inboard lashed position, and the gunports are held closed by hooks that pass through a crossbar and are then screwed tight. The mess plates are accurately drawn and the mess numbers can be seen on some plates. The upturned bread barge at the extreme left is spilling out its stock of ship's biscuits. The marine on his knees, lower centre, has dropped his net, which was used for carrying boiled vegetables or 'duff' pudding. Mess 'kettles' are also shown; the one in the centre is hung in its correct position above the end of the table, while the one lower left has spilt its contents. On the bulkhead can be seen crockery racks, a mirror, and a calendar. In the distance a ramrod and sponge are falling from their stowed positions on the deckhead.

Working the ship

Seamen new to *Warrior* found that, though the deckhead was higher and men no longer cracked their heads on the low beams, she was simply a scaled up version of a wooden ship. They still had to do things the old way – and the old way was to use muscle power.

They handled the sails and the guns, and left the engines to the engineers and stokers. But they could not leave the re-fuelling to the small band of engineers; this was a task where every hand had to help as hard and fast as he could.

Coaling

The ship's coal supply was stowed in eight bunkers set along the side of the machinery spaces, and these were filled by scuttles on the main and lower decks. The total capacity was 850 tons. Using her ten boilers and steaming at full speed the consumption was about 12½ tons per hour, giving approximately 68 hours' steaming, or about 1,000 miles before the coal ran out.

The only sane way to take on coal was to get it over as quickly as possible, and, as steam became more common in the navy, ships competed with each other for the fastest time, recording from start to finish with a stop watch. All hands, including officers, turned to. The band played stirring quick-tempo music as clouds of black dust rose from the ship.

When it was all over the hands manned the pumps to wash down the whole ship.

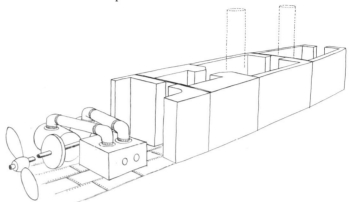

Bunker spaces ran fore and aft almost encircling the boiler rooms. The air temperature beside the boilers was recorded as 92°F and at the fore end the temperature ranged between 82°F and 129°F.

Coaling the ship, late 1860s. The bagged coal was brought alongside and hauled up and in through the gunports. It was dragged inboard and hurried along on trolleys to the coal scuttles, where the bags were emptied. To the extreme left and right of the picture can be seen the guns, covered with canvas to keep out the dust. Within a short time the whole of the gun deck and lower deck would have turned black, the areas between the ports where the men normally ate and slept would have suffered most. The sketch shows that the tables and benches were removed for coaling, but a crockery rack is still clearly visible in the centre of the picture.

Supplying the guns

Unknown to the gunners of *Warrior*, their method of bringing powder cartridges from the magazine to the guns was laying the foundations for a supply system which, when mechanised, was to serve the warships of the twentieth century. In the past the young 'powder monkey' ran down ladderways until he reached the magazine, had his cases filled, and then ran back to his gun. *Warrior*'s system, based on a French idea, was more efficient. Each deck above the magazine had an enclosed area with its own light room. The full cases were handed up through holes in the decks until they reached the gundeck. Returning empty cases were dropped down a canvas chute to land at the magazine entrance. The rate of supply from each supply scuttle had to be no less than 15 to 18 cartridges per minute; thus with two magazines, each with two scuttles, the rate would be at least 60 per minute.

Since the round and elongated shot were stored in garlands on the lower and main decks no special shot store had to be opened during action stations. After any action the shot that had been used was replaced from the central shot locker. Filled shells, round and elongated, were stored in special central shell rooms, and were hauled up by tackle and then carried by hand to the guns.

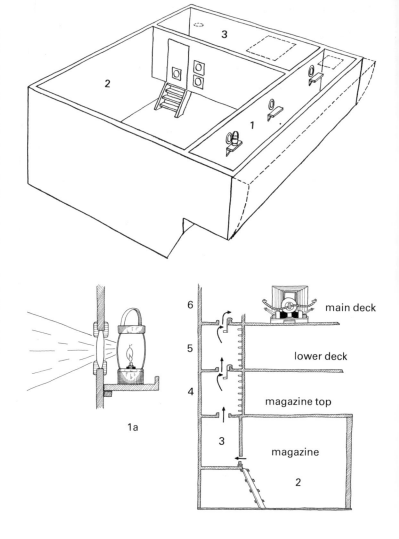

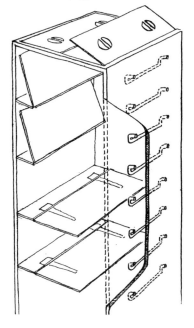

Central shot lockers. These are situated amidships (pp.24–5) and appear as two hatches on the lower deck. When opened, they reveal a vertical shaft reaching to the bottom of the ship. Iron rungs form a ladder on one side. Shelves on the other are used to store shot, hinged so that as each is emptied it can be folded back to expose the next layer below.

The after magazine – port side.
1 *Light gallery. This gallery, lined with copper, runs the length of the magazine. Oil lamps were set on brackets and shone through sealed glass ports (1a) into the main magazine.*
2 *Magazine. Wooden ledges and shelves held large brass cartridge cases, each holding nine cartridges.*
3 *Magazine entrance area. Empty cases were fed by a canvas chute to this level, then by hand through ports into the magazine. Full cases passed from the magazine into the entrance and then up through hand-up holes (4, 5, 6) to the gun deck.*

New ideas in communication

Engine telegraph

The days when the captain sent a midshipman to 'Tell the engine driver to stop!' had given way to hand signals and these in turn gave way to voice pipes. Voice pipes were not ideal in a noisy engine room, and a mechanical telegraph had now been developed. Original plans of *Warrior* show telegraphs on the outboard end of each conning bridge, and these can reasonably be interpreted as engine room telegraphs operated by a handle. The only two known sketches of the engine room show clearly the face of a telegraph (p.9). Evidence remaining on board consists only of holes to carry chains or wires; no bell system or other information, such as whether the mechanism allowed the engineer to acknowledge the signal, has been found.

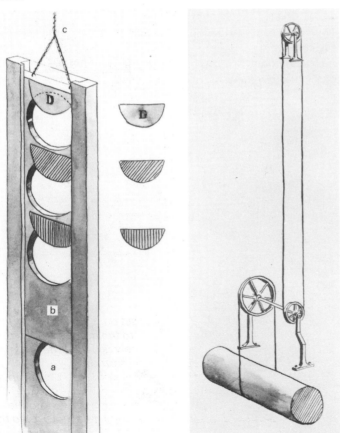

left: *Engine tell-tale.* Even if the engineers had a response mechanism built into the telegraph, the captain had no way of knowing that his orders were being carried out correctly. He could hear, and feel, when the engines were stopped or started up, but that was all. The difficulty was overcome by a simple tell-tale, a wheel in a stand on the upper deck that was connected directly to the propeller shaft. Since the maximum number of revolutions per minute was 55, and in practice much less than this, it was easy to see at a glance whether the engines were going ahead or astern and roughly at what speed. It is very probable that 'Warrior' had a tell-tale, though no positive evidence exists. The photograph above is of a tell-tale on 'Zealous', 1862.

far left: *Magazine telegraph.* The safety precautions which isolated the magazine in almost air-tight conditions in the bowels of the ship made quick communication very difficult. However, since only a few familiar orders were necessary, a simple magazine telegraph could be used. On the gun deck, the officer passing the order simply pulled a rope and set it in a notch in a vertical board. In the magazine entrance area, the rope moved a board vertically in front of the light port. The holes in the board allowed light to pass, but each had a coloured glass section indicating a different order. When the board was moved the sections between the holes naturally blocked the light for a second, and this indicated that a change of orders was coming.

   a Light port
   b Movable board with three holes
   c Rope leading to main deck

Glass hung down over the holes: blue meant 'full charges', red 'reduced charges'. The top glass was clear but had a large D painted on it, meaning 'distance firing'. When the board was hauled right up and clear of the port, this indicated 'cease firing'.

The pumps

The twelve hand-operated Downton pumps were mostly situated on the lower deck. They could be used either for draining the bilges or for fire-fighting. They were turned by long handles capable of taking twelve men. Some had a spindle connecting to the main deck where 48 men could man the handles. These main deck arrangements are still present on *Warrior*.

Hauling in the anchor cable

To raise the anchor about 120 men manned the bars and swifters of the upper deck capstan, and stamped round and round, encouraged by music from the band. The upper capstan was connected directly to the capstan below it on the main deck. The messenger chain, 1⅝-inch studded cable, was taken three times round the lower capstan, along the deck forward, and back down the other side of the ship to the capstan. It was

Downton pump

guided by rollers at key points and formed an endless revolving chain.

The main anchor cable, of 2⅜-inch studded link chain, lay along the deck beside the messenger. The cable and messenger were nipped together at intervals and so the messenger dragged the main cable aft.

The messenger system
1 Capstan on upper deck, turned by crew manning capstan bars.
2 Lower capstan on main deck, set in motion by 1.
3 Endless messenger chain; runs round capstan, along deck to bows, round rollers and back to capstan.
4 Rollers to guide messenger.
5 Main anchor chain cable; leads from hawse pipe forward, along deck and then down Spurling gate to chain lockers below.
6 Spurling gate and pipe to chain locker.
7 Chain or rope lashings (shown in detail on inset) held by nipper men to bind cable to messenger and so drag it aft. The nipper men must release the lashings before reaching the Spurling gate, and then hurry forward to repeat the procedure.

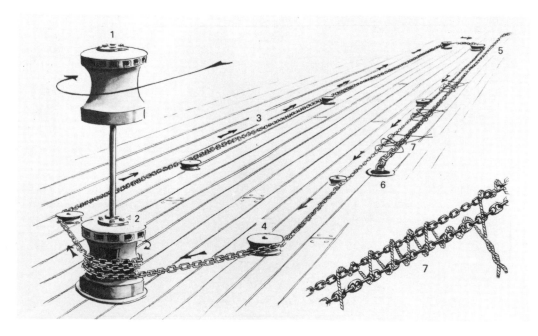

Steering

The screw well (p.10) was placed centrally and immediately in front of the rudder post, so a straight single tiller could not be used ; a yoke, or crosshead tiller, had to be fitted to the rudder post with its arms stretching across the ship until they cleared the screw well. Through a series of blocks and tackles, steering ropes made of leather thongs led forward to the quadruple steering wheels, 6 feet in diameter.

Probably because the designers did not fully understand the need for a new form of rudder in ships modified for a propeller, it was found that Warrior was a brute to steer. This was a problem all her life. Although it was intended that four quartermasters could manage the wheels, she often had between eight and sixteen men hauling on the spokes, and sometimes groups of men working relieving tackles on the crosshead tiller. Steering was to remain a problem for the new generation of ships that was to follow Warrior.

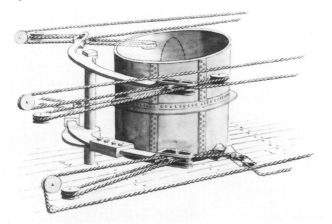

The policy of keeping fleets in tight formation while performing complicated manoeuvres made the ships of the Victorian navy a menace to each other. Warrior, like many others, had an accident; in 1868 she ran into the stern of the ship ahead, the Royal Oak. Fortunately the collision caused only superficial damage, but she did lose her figurehead. It fell onto the quarterdeck of Royal Oak, whose officers immediately seized it as a trophy. Careful examination of the photographs of the figurehead before and after 1868 show differences, which suggests that the original was never regained and that a new one had to be carved.

Expectations

In 1860 everyone in Britain knew about HMS Victory: that she had been commissioned in 1758, that at the age of nearly fifty she had carried Nelson into the carnage of Trafalgar, that she had been visited by the Queen in 1844, and that she was now over one hundred years old. If such was the lifespan of a wooden ship, what then was the fighting life expectancy of this new, far stronger, iron ship? Most people, unaware of the events set in motion by the building of Warrior, naturally presumed that in the 1900s she would still be one of Britain's foremost battleships. Not even the most pessimistic could have envisaged how short her active life span was to be.

Steering gear
1 Upper crosshead tiller
2 Lower crosshead tiller
3 Sheaves for tiller ropes set inside stern bulkhead
4 Screw well
5 Upper deck steering wheels
6 Main deck steering wheels

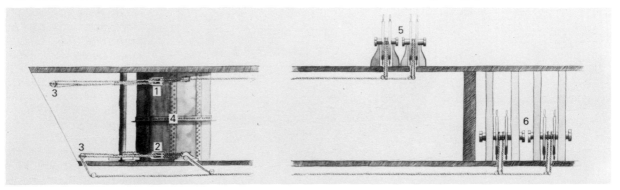

4 Left behind by progress

Technology on the move

The logic of defensive armour, big guns, and speed which created *Warrior* now took on a momentum of its own. Any nation could, knowing now that it was possible, build an iron warship, but with thicker armour. The reply to this would be to mount even bigger guns, though a ship could not carry so many. The race between guns and armour was now on. Meanwhile pressure of steam for the engines, which had seemed so remarkable at 22 pounds per square inch, rose in a few years to 50 pounds and went on increasing. Engine efficiency and size developed at the same rate.

Many nations started building or buying ironclads with ever-thickening armour and ever-growing guns. Wooden warships were now a thing of the past; at best merely stop-gaps until an ironclad fleet could be built.

The earlier misgivings of many in the Admiralty had turned into a nightmare. This one ship had suddenly relegated the rest of the British navy to scrapwood. Britain now had no option but to set about changing her entire battlefleet. The only consolation was that she was ahead in experience, and had greater wealth and industrial resources than any other nation.

Soon the backbone of the late Victorian navy was formed of black-hulled iron ships – the so called 'black battlefleet'. *Warrior* had her few years of glory and then faded from the limelight. By 1865 she was no longer being mentioned in the newspapers, and in 1871 she was no longer classed as a first-line battleship. It had taken only ten years for her to be pushed aside by the developments she herself had done most to accelerate.

ALAN B CHESLEY

The American Civil War, Sunday 9 March 1862.

In Hampton Roads the Confederate 'Virginia' (the ex-Union 'Merrimac', a wooden ship now iron armoured) steamed amongst a Union fleet of wooden warships causing heavy damage and chaos. Next day the Union 'Monitor' arrived to challenge her. The 'Monitor' was a specially designed iron-hulled and iron-armoured ship with a single turret. An extremely noisy but mainly ineffective battle took place with both ships firing away for over two hours before calling it off.

Neither side had suitable ammunition for such a battle but the rest of the world now assumed that an ironclad could, with impunity, shatter a wooden fleet – and it could only be stopped by another ironclad. This first battle of ironclads silenced all critics of iron ships.

The forgotten ship

After a refit in 1871, *Warrior* became part of the reserve fleet. In 1883 she was withdrawn from seagoing service and became forgotten and neglected. At the turn of the century she was on sale for scrap, but no one wanted her. She spent two years as a depot ship and in 1904 became *Vernon III*, part of the Vernon Torpedo Training Establishment at Portsmouth.

In 1924 she was again offered for scrap, but still no one wanted her. In 1929 she became Oil Fuel Hulk C77 and was used as a jetty at Pembroke Dock Oil Fuel Depot.

Her part in transforming the warships of the world, from the white-sailed three-deckers of Trafalgar to the turreted grey steel fortresses of Jutland, found only casual reference in a few history books. The most important ship in that transformation, the one that both contained the past and displayed the shape of the future, remained afloat only because nobody would buy her as scrap and because her hull was still strong enough for hard work.

above: *The Vernon Torpedo Training School. This photograph, taken about 1920, shows two stages of naval evolution, long obsolete, still making a humble contribution to the needs of a later generation. On the right 'Marlborough', once the pride of the 'wooden walls' but now Vernon II, rises above 'Warrior' (Vernon III) on the far left. Between them lies 'Donegal' (Vernon I), a second-rate wooden ship. The two old style wooden hulls rest with the ship that made them obsolete, herself now obsolete too. Shorn of her masts and rigging, 'Warrior' serves only as a power house to provide steam and electricity for the hulks beside her.*

right: *Oil Fuel Hulk C77 in 1978. Here 'Warrior' is seen as a jetty. Ships tied up to her starboard side and received oil from pipelines that came from high tanks and crossed 'Warrior's' decks. Still under Admiralty control, she was drydocked and checked at regular intervals. By now all other Victorian battleships had either sunk or gone to the shipbreakers – only 'Warrior' still clung to life.*

The domino effect: guns and armour

The failure in the late 1860s of the breech mechanism of the large breech-loaders caused the navy to revert to muzzle-loaders, though these were given rifled barrels. It was not until 1881 that a satisfactory breech mechanism came into operation.

The drawings below, made about 1873, indicate how guns grew in size. The larger the guns, the fewer could be carried on a ship, and this was probably the most important factor in the changing design of warships,

The increasing size of guns in the ten years after 'Warrior' came into service

1860 68-pounder, 95-hundredweight smooth-bore muzzle-loader

1865 9-inch (250-pound shell) 12-ton rifled muzzle-loader

1868 10-inch (400-pound shell) 18-ton rifled muzzle-loader

1868 12-inch (600-pound shell) 25-ton rifled muzzle-loader

1872 12-inch (600-pound shell) 30-ton rifled muzzle-loader

The size of rifled muzzle-loading naval guns increased to 16-inch bore before the return of the breech-loaders. Efficient breech-loaders of 12-inch bore were in use in the early 1880s, and this remained the approximate size for several years since new developments in quality rather than size made the shells more effective at piercing armour.

"The 'British tar' of the future" and *"Vulcan crowning Neptune"*. *These two cartoons from 'Punch' show two sides of public awareness of the ironclad ship. They appeared in two successive issues in April 1862. The first, though mainly intended as fun, does not seem entirely impressed with new developments. The second, where no humour seems to be intended, shows John Bull as the invulnerable king of the sea.*

The design of ships changed rapidly once *Warrior* had led the way. Every advance was countered by another – mainly in the battle between size of gun and thickness of armour. Masts altered and sails disappeared as engines became more reliable and as bunkering ports for coal, and later oil, were established throughout the world.

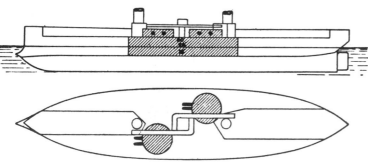

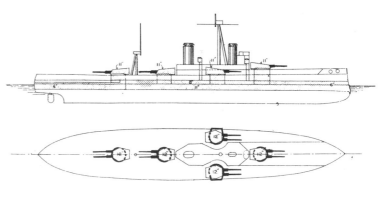

Twenty years' progress – HMS 'Inflexible', launched 1876, completed 1881. She carried the heaviest muzzle-loading guns (16-inch, 80-ton, firing a 1,684 lb shell) and the heaviest armour (two layers of iron with wood backing giving a total thickness of 41 inches). Her armour formed a citadel occupying 110 feet of her 320-foot length, but her massive guns, there were only four, revolved in two turrets and had to be lowered for loading. Her masts were of little use except for signals and her speed of 14.75 knots came from her engines alone. The first captain of 'Inflexible' was J.A. Fisher – the one time gunnery officer of 'Warrior'.

Forty years' progress – HMS 'Dreadnought', launched 1906, completed 1906. She was the first of a new type of fighting ship, the 'all-big-gun ship'. Her ten 12-inch guns were mounted in pairs in turrets. Her turbine engines gave her a speed of 21 knots. It was J.A. Fisher, now the First Sea Lord, who ordered her to be built. 'Warrior' had come into existence because of a challenge from France, and 'Dreadnought' was to meet a challenge from Germany. Like 'Warrior' she never had to fire a shot in anger, but caused a revolution in battleship design and made earlier ships obsolete. From this date large warships were classed as either 'Dreadnought' or 'pre-Dreadnought'.

5 *Warrior* returns

Rescue

In 1979 *Warrior*'s slide into oblivion was reversed when she was handed over to the Maritime Trust for restoration to her original condition. In September of that year she was towed around the coast and berthed at the Coal Dock, Hartlepool, County Cleveland. A restoration team was established and shipyard workers, mainly from the recently closed local shipyards, were recruited as the workforce. Work began on clearing away the additions of a century. *Warrior* was now nearly 120 years old, and a new, more promising, phase of her life began.

1874

1979

1979

'Warrior' as a sea-going warship (1874) with her funnels in the lowered position, and as a hulk awaiting repair at Hartlepool (1979). A glance is sufficient to show how much work has to be done on the rigging, but her hull remained wonderfully sound. Despite the ravages of time the water in the bilges was either rainwater or condensation; after 120 years her hull had not let in a drop of seawater.

1982

On 'Warrior's' arrival at Hartlepool the upper deck was found to be covered with a layer of concrete, averaging 6 inches deep. There were also lampposts, walls, and a helicopter pad. Road drills had to be used to remove the 250 tons of concrete before the iron deck plates and strengtheners stood out clear, many in an excellent state of preservation.

1981

1874

1982

1982

While she was a jetty 'Warrior's' bow was damaged by another ship and part of the fine beak was knocked off. This was recovered from the sea and retained for reconstruction. The crumpled iron can be clearly seen in the photograph of March 1981. A new beak, retaining as much as possible of the old, was fitted in 1981. The broad white line is modern. 'Warrior' never had the white chequered streak of earlier frigates.

The old figurehead had been retained ashore at Portsmouth, but over the years it had slowly deteriorated and was finally burnt. It weighed about 5 tons and fitted over the beak (left). Using sketches and photographs, like the 1874 one shown, Jack Whitehead and Norman Gaches, of the Isle of Wight, set about the task of recarving the 12ft high armoured figure. They can be seen at work on the early stages in 1982 (above).

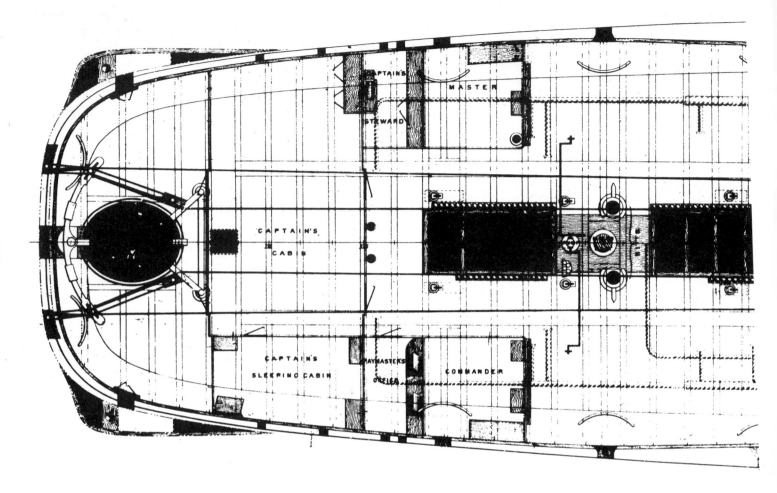

The main deck, aft. It was the practice among Victorian draughtsmen that items immediately below the deck were also shown in the drawing. The sets of parallel lines indicate the beams beneath the deck and the black horizontal lines, four of them, are the tiller ropes which emerge at deck level beside the tiller and propeller shaft.

This section of the ship was unarmoured and the dark areas on the side of the ship are port holes and gunports, and two of them are the doors into the gallery. The square just forward of the propeller shaft is the hatch leading down to the captain's storeroom, the larger rectangle to the right is the hatch above the wardroom.

The dotted lines through the master's and commander's cabins show the ventilating pipe in the wardroom cabins below.

Ship's plans

The most important of all sources of information for the re-construction of *Warrior* were the original ship's plans. These detailed, accurate and beautifully drawn plans are often in colour and could be considered as works of art. However, there is more than one set of plans, and care had to be exercised in their use. There is the first set showing the ship 'as intended'; then the 'as fitted' set; then many more showing alterations, and sometimes they are not dated. All plans had to be carefully examined and then compared with the ship itself before any restoration work could safely begin.

Reconstruction below decks

Once the upper deck had been cleared and made watertight work could start below. Replicas of the guns and their wooden carriages were to be placed in each gun bay and the area between each pair of guns would need its table, benches, crockery rack and all the impedimenta for serving the guns. After about six months of research and analysing all the screw holes and paint marks throughout the main deck, work on the restoration started in 1982. The present visible record was compared with all available information from the past, including standard procedures and regulations of 1860–2, and plans were drawn up for the first reconstructed gun and mess area.

On the lower deck various alterations made in the early 1900s had to be undone. This meant some heavy rebuilding of deck plating, bunker areas and casings. By the end of 1982 the heavy repair work was nearing completion and it was possible to see *Warrior* taking on the appearance she had had 120 years before.

Early 1981. The deckhead and wooden bulkhead have been carefully cleaned to reveal all the original holes and marks. Some of the first replacements were the hammock hooks and these can be seen in the beams. The circular hole high on the bulkhead is a small ventilating tube leading into the upper deck bulwarks. The modern hammock is for demonstration purposes.

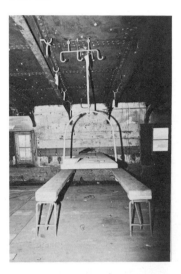

February 1982. The large eyes for the gun tackle can be seen in the bulkhead at the sides of the gunports. The mess table and benches are in position and above can be seen the hooks for the ramrods and sponges. The hooks on the beam to the left are for a rope, ramrod and sponge.

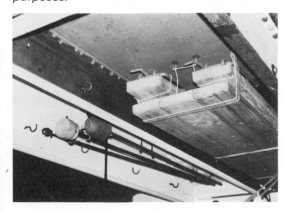

June 1982. The ramrod, worm and sponge (without its sheepskin covering) are in position and the table and benches lashed in their stowed positions, leaving the deck clear for operating the guns.

June 1982. The hammock is in the same position as on the first photograph and the whole area has been cleaned and painted and a bread bin added. On the bulkhead above the table the crockery rack stands empty except for a cutlery tray.

Research on small items

Much of the work on *Warrior* depended on the study of small details and it was structured like an archaeological excavation. Areas were examined carefully, and all items found were photographed and labelled before being moved. Woodwork was checked for screw holes and paintwork for fine paint ridges – anything that might indicate that 120 years ago there had been a fixture of some sort.

Another branch of research was to investigate what sketches, photographs, and official records could tell about equipment and fittings of the 1860–2 period – swords, rifles, bayonets, pistols, cutlasses, lamps, galley utensils and so on. All such items, or at least replicas, must take their correct place in the completed ship.

Colt rack. Hidden away in recesses, corners, and unused areas of the ship there remained many of the original fittings; these serve as indicators to what is missing elsewhere. Above is one of the pistol racks above a gun bay, complete with hooks to hold a revolver. A replica Colt was tested on the rack, and it clicked securely into place.

Mess plate and bowls. Wooden plates and bowls had given way to metal ones, though ceramic and enamelled equipment may have been introduced on 'Warrior'. Whatever style was in use, all articles would have had the mess number clearly marked on them. Any breakages or losses would have had to be paid for by the seamen.

Each seaman was entitled to one plate, one bowl and one spoon. Sets of much finer ware were supplied to the wardroom and senior officers.

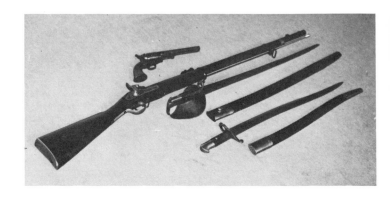

Replicas of the 1858 sea service Enfield rifle and the sea service Colt revolver, with actual examples of the cutlass-bayonet and the marine artillery sword bayonet.

Each gun bay had four cutlasses and a Colt revolver in racks, and there were over 200 rifles in the main-deck racks. Since Colts were officially withdrawn in 1860 'Warrior' may have been the last navy vessel to carry them.

Midshipman Murray's log

It was not difficult to obtain information about the construction of the body of the ship, because so much remained intact and the splendid original plans were still available (p.44). But how could the restorers know exactly where all the various movable pieces of equipment and stores were positioned? Admiralty regulations, for example, might sometimes give guidance about where these things were generally kept, but this left a great deal to guesswork. The situation was saved by Midshipman Murray – or rather the plans he drew for his logbook in 1862. One copy was preserved in the Royal Naval Museum, Portsmouth and another copy was discovered in the Captain's Letter Book which belonged to Captain Cochrane. Murray sketched all the decks of *Warrior* and noted where all items were stored. This active fourteen-year-old boy, as far as anyone can tell, had every reason for trying to get everything right and none for misrepresenting anything. His evidence soon proved to be the most valuable aid the restorers could have in their attempt to recreate in detail the life of *Warrior*.

Henry Arthur Keith Murray, Born 1847. He joined the navy in 1860 and served on 'Warrior' as a midshipman from September 1861 to March 1863. Resigned from the navy in 1872 as a lieutenant. He settled in Virginia, USA, where he married; a daughter was born in 1878. After the death of his wife in 1899 he returned to Britain. In 1914, at the age of 67, he offered his services for World War I but was not accepted. He died in 1918, aged 71.

Date of photograph unknown: probably taken when he was in his early twenties. Part of his plans is shown below.

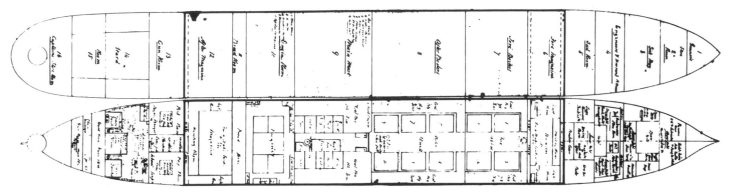

This model of 'Warrior' is in the Science Museum, London, and probably dates from when she was being built at the Thames Iron Works, Blackwall. The original drawings of 'Warrior' show the figurehead holding a scimitar, as it does in the model. All evidence available clearly shows that when she was commissioned the scimitar had become a straight sword, which strongly suggests that this model was made about 1859–60.

It is an eyecatching and impressive model and, though lacking in the fine detail needed for full scale reconstruction work, it gives the restorers an excellent idea of what the final result of their efforts will be.

The lucky ship

After all the twists and turns of fate, and thanks largely to her rust-resistant wrought-iron hull, *Warrior* is still afloat, and is now being preserved for the benefit of many generations to come. In her heyday she was always considered a lucky ship and never had to fire a gun in anger. Perhaps that is why she has not, until now, loomed large in the memory and imagination of the public. *Warrior* has no fallen hero whose blood stained her decks, and she took part in no famous battles; her presence alone cowed potential enemies for a few years, and then her successors took over. After a mere decade, *Warrior* fell into obscurity. After a century of neglect, though, she emerges to become famous again.

Warrior is outstanding not only for her size and complex structure, not only for all the revolutionary features inherent within her, and not only because she is the only surviving Victorian battleship, but because she acted upon the pattern of history by simply existing. From the time of *Gloire* and *Warrior* to the time of the nuclear submarines, international power politics have depended heavily on possessing large ships that are technically more advanced than those of any potential enemy. Overwhelming superiority may ensure peace, as *Warrior* did. It may also provoke competition in developing bigger and better armaments, as *Warrior* also did.

Warrior is saved to become a national treasure, a monument of British inventiveness, industry and workmanship in the Victorian age. Equally she reminds us of the vision and enterprise of the Frenchman Dupuy de Lôme, who, with his *Gloire*, forced the reluctant British Admiralty to lead the naval revolution.

Perhaps the best way to end is to say simply that she was the ship that changed them all.